MW01515943

Rab,
Greyfriars Bobby,
Fiddy &
Fan

Rab

The country folk living in Newlands Parish, Midlothian were absolutely terrified. A big grey dog had been worrying the sheep grazing in the district. Although the local landowner had issued orders for the dog to be captured, the bull mastiff was still at large as no one had the courage to approach the big grey beast.

Just as the landowner was about to send back to his house for his shotgun, a horse drawn cart arrived on the scene driven by John Jackson. The carter made his living by collecting poultry, eggs, cheese and butter from the local farms which he delivered to the Edinburgh markets.

Managing to grab hold of the dog, John tied a rope around the struggling animal's neck and dragged him back to his cart. Hitching the rope to the vehicle's tailboard, John set off for his cottage at Howgate which lay two miles south of Penicuik.

John's wife Margaret spotted the cart in the distance as it trundled down the road from Leadburn. She had guessed that something had held John up as he liked to set off in plenty of time for the town.

Unable to see the dog tethered behind, Margaret could not figure why Jess was having difficulty pulling the cart. The grey mare looked exhausted as the dog who weighed nearly ninety pounds had been dragging on the rope during the journey.

Arriving at the cottage, John jumped down from the driving seat, annoyed at being behind schedule. As he untied the dog Margaret took a look at the large brindled animal. The mastiff had a huge head while his mouth and muzzle were jet black. The grey hairs on his coat were short and stiff. He looked like a small Highland bull which had been carved from Aberdeen granite.

Taking a look at the dog's paws, Margaret spotted the reason for his aggressive behaviour. A splinter of wood was sticking in his foreleg causing him a lot of pain. John had no time to hang about. Anxious to be on his way, he quickly got up on the driving seat. Flicking his whip at Jess's hindquarters he set off for the capital.

Filling a bowl with water for the mastiff to drink, Margaret managed to persuade the dog to stick his paw through a gap at the bottom of a door. With the dog safely on the opposite side in case he attacked her while she was on the other, Margaret quickly removed the splinter. Opening the door slightly she pushed a plate of meat through the narrow gap and quickly shut it.

Taking a peek when she decided it was safe enough, Margaret found a completely different dog from the animal who had arrived at Loanstone cottage earlier that day. No longer suffering from the pain in his leg, now that he had been fed and allowed to take a nap the mastiff was a new animal. Grateful to Margaret for removing the splinter, the big grey dog laid his giant head affectionately on Mrs. Jackson's lap.

When John returned from Edinburgh he found that the dog who had been causing so much trouble was now quite tame. The couple had no family as their only daughter had died in childhood. Deciding that the mastiff would make a good watchdog and be company for John on his trips to Edinburgh the couple decided to keep him.

Quickly settling into the Jacksons' routine, Rab accompanied the carter on his trips to the markets. While John was hitching Jess to the cart, Rab would trot into the cottage. Full of importance he would pad up to Mrs. Jackson to let her know that the carter would be in at any minute to say goodbye before setting off for the city.

One day when John was returning from Edinburgh as he was approaching Auchendinny village, a man suddenly jumped out into the roadway and demanded the carter's cash.

Promising to hand it over, John gave Rab an order as he climbed down from the cart. Quick as a flash the mastiff leapt at the villain and knocked him over. Pinning him to the ground, Rab's bared teeth warned him that it would be his unlucky day if he moved a muscle.

Jumping back into the driving seat, John flicked his whip at Jess and quickly headed for Howgate at a fast trot leaving Rab standing guard over his terrified prisoner. As John looked back over his shoulder, he was amused to see the layabout being forced back to the ground every time he tried to get up.

As John was explaining to his wife how Rab had saved him from being robbed, the mastiff trotted up to the cottage. The carter later discovered that the would be villain was the son of a neighbour which explained why Rab had not torn him apart. Recognising the rogue, the mastiff had decided to let him off lightly.

One day in 1824 after John had made his weekly delivery to the Grassmarket, he had driven as usual up Candlemaker Row to the

Harrow Inn which stood close to Greyfriars Kirk. While the carter was wetting his whistle and enjoying the crack in the busy smoke filled tavern, Rab decided to take a walk along the Cowgate.

Although Rab was not aggressive, city regulations required that dogs had to be muzzled. John did not want to be stopped by the police and given a fine so Rab was wearing a muzzle.

As the grey mastiff was making his way under the massive arch of the South Bridge, he spotted a white bull terrier trotting towards him. Not only was the cocky wee beast not wearing a muzzle, he was looking for trouble as he had just defeated a Border collie in a scrap near the Tron Kirk.

The terrier suddenly jumped at Rab and gripped the mastiff by the throat. As his jaws were strapped together, Rab was unable to defend himself from the terrier's attack.

Two High School pupils, fourteen year old John Brown and Bob Ainslie had witnessed the fight between the terrier and the collie at the Tron and had followed the little devil as he trotted down Niddry Street looking for another dog to fight.

As the terrier hung on to Rab's throat a mob gathered to watch the scrap. Realising that the mastiff would not stand a chance as he was muzzled, Bob borrowed a knife from one of the spectators. He handed the cobbler's knife to John who grabbed the muzzle and quickly cut through one of the leather straps holding Rab's jaws together.

Although he was not aggressive by nature, Rab was a bonnie fechter. Wasting no time he quickly despatched his attacker who had bitten off more than he could chew. As Rab left the scene the boys picked up the terrier's body for burial. Curious to find out who the mastiff belonged to, they followed Rab back along the Cowgate as the big grey dog headed for the Harrow Inn.

John Jackson was standing outside the tavern holding the reins of his horse as he scanned the street for his dog. Assuming that Rab had been stolen, the carter tried to hide the fact that he was glad to see him by shouting at the mastiff.

Calming down after the boys explained what had happened,

John jumped up on the cart and headed home to Howgate.

After leaving school John Brown enrolled at Edinburgh University. Deciding he would like to become a surgeon, the eighteen year old student was apprenticed to James Syme who ran a training hospital at Minto House on the city's south side.The hospital which contained twenty four beds stood in Argyle Square overlooking the Cowgate.

When John and Rab came into the town, usually on a Wednesday the mastiff never failed to head for the hospital to see if his friend had managed to find him a juicy bone. Leaving Jess standing outside and the carter inside the Harrow Inn, Rab trotted up Candlemaker Row, past Greyfriars Kirk and turned left towards Argyle Square.

As the years passed and Rab faithfully continued to turn up at Minto House, John noted that when the big grey dog trotted through the hospital gate he usually had the marks of yet another battle on his sturdy body.

Rab now only had one eye and two teeth while his giant head was covered with scars gained over the years in canine scraps. Part of an ear was missing, his other lug looked like a tattered old battle flag and his tail was now only about an inch long.

When Margaret Jackson was approaching her fiftieth birthday she began to feel unwell. As the pain in her breast continued to increase, John decided to take his wife to Minto House for treatment. Margaret was examined by the surgeon who recommended that she should be operated on immediately.

Watched by the carter, Rab and over 200 medical students, the surgeon quickly went to work assisted by John Brown. Although Margaret seemed to have pulled through, the operation was unsuccessful and she died a few days later.

John who had stayed on at the hospital to nurse his wife was heart broken. Returning to the cottage, he hitched Jess to the cart and drove back to Edinburgh. Carefully wrapping his wife's body in a blanket, John drove back to Howgate. Margaret was buried at St. Mungo's Church at Penicuik on a cold winter's day in December 1830.

Shortly after the funeral, John fell ill when a fever epidemic hit the area. Already suffering from depression, the forty five year old carter was in no shape to fight the illness and was buried in the same grave as his wife in January the following year.

Although the carter who took over the Jacksons' business also decided to look after Rab, the dog refused to settle down. The old grey mastiff missed the man who had saved him from being shot and his wife who had removed the splinter from his leg.

Tired with life, overweight and crabbit, Rab would stay in the stable with his old friend Jess and refuse to come out. When the carter came in to feed the horse, Rab not only growled at him but tried to take a toothless bite out his leg.

As Rab's aggressive behaviour was not helping his business, the carter had no choice but to put the dog out of his misery. Rab was buried on the braeside near the Howgate burn.

Almost thirty years after Rab's death, John Brown now a successful consultant decided to record the story of the faithful dog who had trotted up the Candlemaker Row to visit him when he was training to be a surgeon.

The surgeon decided to change the names of John and Margaret Jackson to James and Alison Noble. *Rab and his Friends* quickly became a best seller and by 1862, four years after its publication, fifty thousand copies had been bought by the public.

A plaque embossed with Rab's head and dedicated to the memory of the Howgate carter and his wife can be seen at St. Mungo's Church, Penicuik, Midlothian where John and Margaret Jackson are buried.

Fiddy

William Chambers worked as an apprentice bookseller in Edinburgh's Calton Street. His father had run into financial difficulties forcing him to leave William and his young brother Robert to fend for themselves in lodgings at the city's West Port.

As William had to manage on four shillings a week, he had come to an arrangement with a baker. In return for reading stories to the baker's employees during their early morning shift, the youngster received a hot bap straight from the oven.

At the end of his apprenticeship, the nineteen year old opened a book shop in Leith Walk. Saving every penny which had come into the shop, the two brothers had set up a publishing business in the High Street. Ambitious and hard working, the brothers began publishing a weekly magazine. Costing a ha'penny a copy 'Chambers's Journal' had quickly caught on with the public. The circulation had shot up to 80,000 making the brothers very rich men.

Visiting Mrs. Rogers who lived at Stockbridge in the north of the city, William's wife Harriet found that her friend now owned five glossy black and tan pups. The pups' father had been fished out the Water of Leith by children playing on the river bank.

The youngsters had taken the dog to the Rogers' house thinking that the spaniel belonged to the solicitor and his wife. Mrs. Rogers had instructed her housemaid to take the spaniel down to the kitchen in the basement and dry him off. The couple had decided to keep the dog. Mated with a spaniel named Beauty, Tom had fathered the five pups.

The Chambers had no family as their three children had died in infancy. Although Harriet had sworn that she would never own another dog due to the emotional upset it caused when the animal died, she had changed her mind on seeing the beautiful little pups. Knowing that her husband would not object to having a dog in the house, Mrs. Chambers had taken one of the tiny black spaniels back to Manor Place.

The housemaids Christina and Mary were given the job of looking after the little spaniel. Christy immediately made friends with Fiddy treating her like a princess and singing to her as she dressed her up. Wearing an amber bead necklace around her neck while her ears were decorated with coloured ribbons and artificial flowers Fiddy would trot back to the drawing room to show off.

As well as being full of life, Fiddy was also full of curiousity. When out for a walk, she would sometimes trot off to examine any object which attracted her attention. To cure her of the habit, William and Harriet decided to send her to a canine training school at Coltbridge on the western outskirts of the city.

The canine academy took in every breed from tiny terriers to giant Newfoundlands. Although the trainer did not ill treat his four legged pupils, he was a strict disciplinarian and did not hesitate to use his whip if they failed to respond to his whistle. He also disapproved of dogs who were overweight and did not believe in overfeeding them.

Two weeks after the little dog had been at the establishment, William visited the school to see how Fiddy was progressing. The publisher found that she had picked up a few bad habits from a terrier she had become friendly with. The well behaved dog from the city's west end now growled at anyone who came near her when she was gnawing at a bone.

In addition to looking as if she needed a good feed, William was not happy with the fact that Fiddy was associating with the terrier. Picking the little dog up, the publisher paid the trainer his three shilling fee and took Fiddy back home.

Harriet almost fainted when she saw how much weight the spaniel had lost. Fiddy was given two biscuits as an appetiser before being served with a plate piled high with juicy bones.

The spaniel liked to occupy the sofa in the drawing room which stood in front of the fireplace. Like all dogs Fiddy thrived on attention and did not believe in keeping a low profile. When she felt she was being ignored, she would get up, walk to the middle of the room and lie down on her side. If she found that her tactics were not working she would bark loudly, beating her tail on the carpet at the same time.

When she was in the kitchen, Fiddy would sit on a table next to the window and keep a look out for cats. If she spotted a puss prowling around the back green, she would bark loudly to raise the alarm before dashing out the door to chase the intruder from her territory.

During the autumn of 1848, the Chambers took Fiddy on holiday with them to Peebles. Staying at a villa, the grey haired publisher took Fiddy for walks in the surrounding countryside. During their stay, the spaniel made friends with a Scottish terrier called Dandy.

One morning Christina took Fiddy with her when she went on an errand to the local green grocer's in Stafford Street not far from Manor Place. While the housemaid was chatting to the shopkeeper, Fiddy decided to trot across the road. When Christina came out the shop she found that Fiddy had disappeared.

Thinking that the dog had decided to return home, Christina hurried back to Manor Place. Finding that Fiddy had not arrived Christina and Mary went out to search for her. Mrs. Chambers immediately sent a message to her husband to tell him that Fiddy had disappeared.

After contacting the police, the publisher arranged for hand bills to be printed offering a five pound reward for the dog's return. Unable to concentrate on work he returned to the area where Fiddy had disappeared to search for the little spaniel.

Reaching Maitland Street he spotted Fiddy who was in a terrible state. The publisher was overjoyed to see her. Picking the panting dog up, he carried Fiddy back to Manor Place.

The following year William purchased Glenormiston mansion near Peebles. Improving the property which had cost him £25,500, he spent a further £10,000 draining the land and building houses for his workers.

Fiddy loved to roam free and explore the estate when the Chambers went down to the mansion on holiday. In addition to commissioning a full size painting of Fiddy mounted in a gold frame to hang in the dining room, the publisher had a mural painted showing her playing in the grounds.

Three years later the publisher and his wife decided to visit the U.S.A. and Canada. When the couple returned they found Fiddy waiting to welcome them at the railway station. The couple had brought a present for the spaniel. In addition to the silver bell attached to her collar Fiddy now wore a gold U.S. dollar.

When Fiddy turned ten her health began to fail. Realising that the spaniel's days were coming to an end, the Chambers decided that it would be a good idea to have her photographed. Fiddy was driven in a pony and trap to a photographer's studio at Innerleithen.

Two photographs were taken, one showing her perched on William's knee, while the other showed her sitting on a chair. As she grew older the little spaniel's condition began to get worse. Fiddy was so ill that she now spent most of her time sleeping and had to be carried up and down stairs.

In 1858 when the Chambers were returning to Edinburgh from Peebles by rail after their summer holiday, the little spaniel passed away. Fiddy was buried close to a rose bush on a green mossy bank on the Glenormiston estate.

The couple commissioned a memorial plaque to Fiddy which was set up in the Chambers Institution at Peebles. The centre had been donated to the town where he had been born by the publisher.

In addition to a main hall for functions the building contained a library, reading room and museum. Fiddy's memorial was set up in a small room housing a collection of animals, birds and geological specimens at the end of the gallery.

William Chambers was elected Lord Provost of Edinburgh in 1865. The couple continued to live at the city's west end although they moved round the corner to a bigger house where two ceremonial lamp posts were set up on the pavement to signify that 13 Chester Street was the residence of the Lord Provost.

Greyfriars Bobby

In 1858 a small dog suddenly took up residence in Greyfriars Kirk's burial ground. The locals called the dog Bobby. Three years later a time gun was set up on the Half Moon Battery at Edinburgh Castle. The gun fired automatically when an electrical signal was sent from the city's observatory on the Calton Hill along an overhead wire over 4,000 feet long to the time gun's clock.

Colour Sergeant Donald MacNab Scott who worked at the Castle lived in lodgings at 28 Candlemaker Row. The building's rear windows looked out on to Greyfriars Kirk's burial ground. Making friends with Bobby, the sergeant treated him regularly to a meal at restaurants in the area including Currie's Eating House in Greyfriars Place.

When Colour Sergeant Scott set off from his lodgings for the Castle, the little dog followed him to the end of George IV Bridge before turning round and trotting back to the Greyfriars area.

Dunfermline born businessman John Traill took over Currie's restaurant in 1862 and changed its name. Bobby got on well with the new owner of Traill's Temperance Coffee House and his family who lived in the stair next door to the restaurant and the dog was always welcome in their flat.

Bobby was in the habit of leaving the burial ground to go for his dinner when the Castle time gun fired at one. Now a local character, people would gather outside the kirk's main gate to see

Bobby heading for the refreshment room to enjoy a steak.

Dogs were popular with the public. Queen Victoria owned several including Scottish terriers while Dr. John Brown's book *Rab and his Friends* was a best seller. Bobby's story was featured in the *Inverness Courier*. The story was picked up by several papers including *The Scotsman* and the Greyfriars Bobby legend began.

The newspaper articles claiming that the terrier was guarding his master's grave turned Bobby from a local character into a national celebrity. In addition to visiting the Castle and Holyrood Palace, tourists came to the Greyfriars district to see the dog who had been featured in the press.

When the Dog Duty Act was introduced in 1867 it reduced the licence fee from twelve shillings to seven. As Bobby seemed to be a stray, the dog was unlicenced. Assuming that John Traill owned the dog as the terrier frequented his coffee shop, proceedings were taken against him by the authorities for the payment of the tax and he was summoned to appear at the Burgh Court.

Although the restaurant owner said he would be glad to pay for the licence he added that he could not be held legally responsible for Bobby as no one knew who owned him or where he had come from. Accepting John Traill's explanation, the sheriff dismissed the case.

Lord Provost William Chambers was a director of the Scottish Society for the Prevention of Cruelty to Animals. The Provost and his wife Harriet had been shattered when their spaniel Fiddy had died the same year Bobby appeared in the Greyfriars area.

To solve the problem the Lord Provost offered to pay the seven shillings. He also bought the little dog a leather collar fitted with a brass plate inscribed with the words 'Greyfriars Bobby from the Lord Provost, 1867, licenced'.

The case was reported in the press making Bobby even more famous. Professional photographers took his picture and he was painted by several artists including Gourlay Steell, Queen Victoria's favourite animal painter. Local photographer John Dickson who had a studio at 3 Bristo Place took Bobby's picture. Mounted on card the small photographs with the dog's legend printed on the reverse were popular with the tourists.

Two years later Angela Burdett-Coutts who was a member of the Ladies' Committee of the Royal Society for the Prevention of Cruelty to Animals travelled up to Edinburgh with her friend Hannah Brown to see the little dog who was now under the Lord Provost's protection.

On a cold November day, Angela took a trip to Greyfriars burial ground with a few friends to see the dog who had been trained by Colour Sergeant Scott to go for his dinner when the One o'clock Gun went off.

When she enquired who the dog belonged to, Angela was told that Bobby had been owned by an Army veteran called Robert Gray. After Robert had died in the Royal Infirmary, Bobby had begun inhabiting Greyfriars kirkyard. Reaching the spot where the dog's owner was said to have been buried, Angela and her friends found that the grave was unmarked.

Returning to her suite in the Balmoral Hotel in Princes Street, Angela wrote a letter to the Town Council asking permission to set up a headstone. Angela received a reply stating that the Council would consider the request, but the information she had been given on who the dog had belonged to would have to be checked out. The gravestone was never erected.

Bobby fell ill and died in January 1872. Helped by a few friends John Traill buried the terrier in a triangular flower plot beneath a tree in front of Greyfriars church. A small headstone carved with Bobby's name was set up over the little dog's grave.

Now a baroness, Angela had not forgotten Bobby, and although she had been unable to persuade the Town Council to erect a headstone for Robert Gray, she wrote again asking for permission to donate a memorial of Bobby to the city.

Receiving the go ahead, Angela arranged for a drinking fountain to be designed. A red granite fountain was erected at the south end of George IV Bridge just across from Greyfriars Kirk. Set up in front of a lamp post, the fountain had a metal cup attached to a chain for the use of thirsty passers by. Dogs were able to drink from the fountain as the pedestal's base was shaped like a trough.

A full size bronze statue of Bobby sculpted by William Brodie R.S.A. stood on top of the pedestal. The fountain was unveiled in November 1873. Although he had been born in Perth, Colour Sergeant Scott continued to live in Edinburgh until the end of his days. The Royal Engineer who had become part of the Greyfriars Bobby legend died at the Royal Infirmary in 1893.

Fan

By the 1860's Torquay had developed from a small fishing village into a fashionable seaside resort. Wealthy celebrities including politicians and foreign royalty regularly visited the town during the summer to relax, socialise and enjoy themselves.

Angela Burdett-Coutts was extremely wealthy having been left a fortune by her Scots grandfather Thomas Coutts the banker. Highly intelligent but unable to enter politics as women were not allowed to vote, Angela assisted by her companion Mrs. Hannah Brown devoted her energies to helping the poor and improving Britain's animal protection laws.

The Cornish resort was also a haven for convalescents who had moved to the town hoping that the sea air would improve their health. Not long after buying a house at St. Marychurch Road, a lady who had moved to the town for health reasons died, leaving her dog Sappho to a local vicar.

Although the clergyman was fond of the pinscher, his duties meant he was rarely at home. As he had very little time to look after the dog, the vicar asked Angela if she would take care of Sappho as she loved animals.

Not long after Sappho arrived at Ehrenberg Hall, Angela's

summer residence overlooking Torbay harbour, the small dog disappeared. Forty eight hours later, Angela and Hannah received news that she had been spotted sitting outside the front door of her old home.

Renamed Fan, the pinscher quickly settled down in her new surroundings. In addition to being given a blue ribbon to wear round her neck, Fan had her own chair and plate so that she could sit at the table to take her meals.

Although Fan was highly intelligent, it usually took her twenty four hours to master a new trick. A biscuit was placed on the table and covered with an upturned drinking glass. To get the biscuit Fan had to knock the glass over with her paw. Unable to perform the trick immediately, after sleeping on it overnight, Fan knocked the glass over the following day.

In addition to many other pets, Angela had a dog called Bill who acted as Fan's bodyguard. When Bill was given a bone he would trot off and bury it. He would then find Fan and take her to see his hidden treasure.

Unlike Fan, Bill did not have a pedigree. Banned from the big house, he slept in the stables. If Bill tried to enter the house, Fan would give him a look which told him he was not welcome.

Although Fan was a lady she was fearless and liked to chase rats. One day when the two dogs were out for a walk, Bill spotted the entrance to a drain pipe. The pipe which ran under the road looked as though it might be full of rats and Bill trotted inside to investigate followed by Fan.

Time passed and as there was no sign of the dogs coming out Angela and her companion began to worry as they were not sure if the pipe was full of water. Assuming that the dogs had drowned they decided to return home.

Dripping wet, the two dogs eventually trotted out the far end Trying hard to hide the fact that she was relieved by Fan's return, Angela gave her a severe ticking off. The following day as Bill was about to go rat hunting, Fan stopped him from getting into trouble.

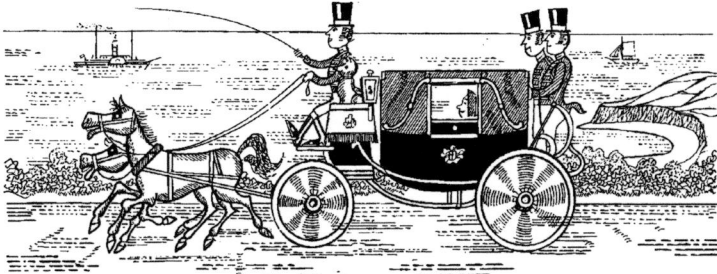

When Angela and Hannah went for a spin in their horse drawn carriage, Fan liked to sit on the driving seat beside the coachman. One day when Fan was out for a walk in a public park with Angela she was attacked by a dog belonging to a young woman.

Hearing Fan barking, the servants who were standing by the carriage quickly rushed to help her. Picking the little dog up, she was carried to the carriage and driven back to Ehrenberg Hall. Although she survived an operation on her shoulder which had been badly mauled, her nervous system had been affected to such an extent by the attack that she lost her sight.

Angela was made a baroness by Queen Victoria in 1871. Although Baroness Burdett-Coutts loved animals she was also aware of their importance to the country's economy. In addition to supplying the finance to build stables for costermongers' donkeys in London, she provided money for setting up horse troughs in the streets of Britain's towns and cities.

That year the Edinburgh Street Tramways Company was given the go ahead to set up a horse drawn tram system which would connect the capital with Leith and Portobello. By November workmen had laid tram rails from Bernard Street at the foot of Leith Walk to Haymarket at the city's west end.

The heavy German built double decker trams were drawn by teams consisting of two horses supplied by Croall's Livery Stables. The horses' collars were fitted with bells and each driver was issued with a whistle to keep the tram lines clear of traffic.

The journey from the bottom of Leith Walk to the General Post Office at the east end of Princes Street lay uphill all the way. The last section leading to Waterloo Place where the Duke of Wellington sat on a bronze horse facing the General Post Office was particularly steep.

To help the teams pull the trams up the slope, trace horses were hitched to the vehicles. In addition to having to stop to take on passengers, the strain on the horses increased when vehicles and bicycles failed to give them the right of way, crossing their path forcing them to stop.

Although the trams were welcomed as an asset to the city, the public soon began to complain about the way the service was being run. The tramcar wheels proved a danger to pedestrians especially along the rail sections running close to the pavement as they were not fitted with protective guards.

The horses were also being overworked and the public was not happy when the company began overloading their trams with too many passengers to increase its profits.

In September 1872 a tram travelling down Leith Street ran out of control overtaking the horses. As the panic stricken animals tried to gallop clear of the runaway vehicle, the horses stumbled and fell outside the Theatre Royal. Careering on, the vehicle crashed into the rear of a tram car standing at Shrubhill half way down Leith Walk.

Two highly qualified experts Charles S. Romanis Inspecting Veterinary Surgeon to H.M. Privy Council and Professor Thomas

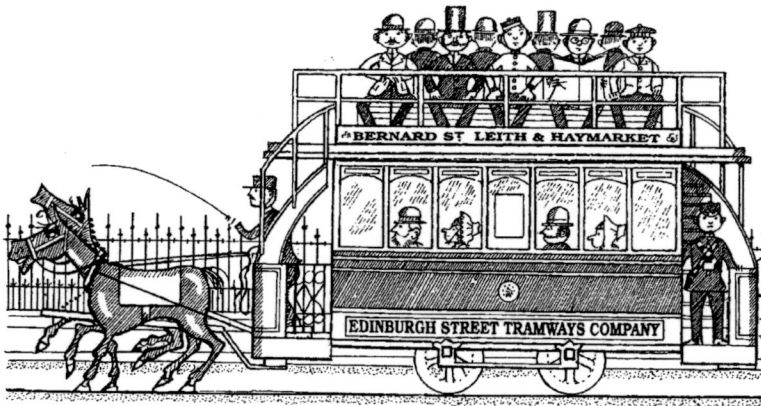

Walley of the Edinburgh Veterinary College were commissioned by the S.S.P.C.A. to produce a report on the company's operations.

Their investigation showed that a quarter of the horses hauling the trams were not fit to carry out the heavy work. To prevent the horses being forced to stop so frequently, the veterinary experts recommended that the police should be instructed to keep the tram lines clear of traffic.

Angela loved to visit Scotland, especially Edinburgh as her grandfather had been Lord Provost of the city. When Baroness Burdett-Coutts paid a visit to the capital the following month she took a trip to Peebles. She was met by William Chambers and the directors of the Chambers Institution who showed her round the building which housed Fiddy's memorial plaque.

When Angela's dog Fan died in May 1872, she decided to write a book aimed at the juvenile market which she hoped would encourage children to be kind to animals.

The following year when she unveiled the drinking fountain dedicated to Greyfriars Bobby, the baroness presented a copy of *Little Fan* to John Traill the restaurant owner who had fed the famous terrier for so many years.

During its campaign to improve the working conditions of Edinburgh's tram horses, the S.S.P.C.A. distributed thousands of leaflets to the public, paid for by Angela who was now President of the R.S.P.C.A.'s Ladies Committee.

Baroness Burdett-Coutts received the Freedom of the City of Edinburgh in January 1874. The ceremony took place in the Music Hall in George Street. The front of the stage was covered with red cloth looped up in folds and decorated with greenhouse plants Two large Union Jack flags were pinned to the wall on either side of the stage.

Surrounded by flags, a painting of Angela's wealthy grandfather

Provost Coutts which she had presented to the city had been set up behind a chair standing in the centre of the stage.

The large hall was packed and in addition to many of the city's dignitaries, the guests included William and Harriet Chambers and William Brodie R.S.A. who had been commissioned by the baroness to sculpt the statue of Greyfriars Bobby.

At one o'clock as the time gun boomed out from the Castle's Half Moon Battery, the members of the Town Council wearing their ceremonial robes filed on to the stage and took their places on the seats set out for them.

When Angela accompanied by Mrs. Brown entered with Lord Provost Cowan, the spectators rose to their feet and gave her a standing ovation. After giving a speech praising Angela's charity work and acknowledging her connection with Edinburgh, Lord Provost Cowan presented the baroness with a silver casket containing the freedom of the city.

That year the Edinburgh Tramway Company cancelled its contract with the livery stables supplying the teams of horses. Purchasing the horses for £28 each, the company gradually began replacing them with sturdier animals.

A new system of working was also introduced closely monitored by the S.S.P.C.A.'s inspectors. Each team now operated on a rota system, the horses spending a period on the less strenuous parts of the line before being transferred to the steeper sections of the network.

Thanks to the work carried out by the S.S.P.C.A. helped by Baroness Burdett-Coutts, the campaign to protect the capital's working horses had proved successful.